ZAPIRO

The Madiba Years

Cartoons from *Sowetan* and the *Mail & Guardian*

FOREWORD BY PIETER-DIRK UYS

To Mum ~ Dad,

Enjoy!

With lots of love from

Isobel ~ Owen.

17ᵗʰ May 1997.

David Philip Publishers
Cape Town & Johannesburg

Acknowledgements: Thanks to my editors at the Mail & Guardian *(Anton Harber, Irwin Manoim) and at* Sowetan *(Aggrey Klaaste, Mike Siluma, Moegsien Williams, Barney Mthombothi, Mike Tissong, Sy Makaringe) for allowing me the artistic freedom to push cartooning boundaries; Karina Turok, Tony Weaver and Liz Fish for many brainstorming sessions; my assistant Greg de Klerk for painstakingly filing my visual references; all at David Philip for their efforts in producing this book at short notice; my parents, siblings and especially my wife Karina for their support of my wacky career choice, even when it was politically and financially risky.*

First published 1996 in southern Africa by
David Philip Publishers (Pty) Ltd,
208 Werdmuller Centre, Claremont 7700
in association with
Karina Turok & Jonathan Shapiro

© 1996 Jonathan Shapiro

ISBN 0-86486-326-8

Cover design by Jonathan Shapiro & Karina Turok
Reproduction by CMYK Pre-press

Printed by Clyson Printers (Pty) Ltd, 11th Avenue, Maitland, 7405, South Africa

Foreword by Pieter-Dirk Uys

I have been cutting out Zapiro's cartoons since I first discovered them. Some of them inspired moments in my shows. Others just made me sigh with envy. Such simplicity and so much substance!

Since I began my minor skirmish against stupid politicians in 1980, I have been primarily inspired by those stupid politicians. But a close second in inspiration came the political cartoonists of the time. They pricked the dinosaur with their pens and made it bleed custard.

The stage revue became my way to shine a torch into the cesspool of politics. Shorthand was the key. Cartooning was the answer. I'm still trying to get to that perfection: using the single line to create multiple lives.

The Struggle Continues! Zapiro ventures where comrades fear to tread! He skates on thin ice, satirising the politically correct and the politically incompetent. Here is a battle plan full of those rare and original insights, where a crisscross of squiggles and shadows reminds us of the sagas of social stupidity and soap operas of political intrigue, that so few tried to hide from so many.

The pen is not just mightier than the sword; here it is lighter to carry, quicker to wield, longer to last, and, for many, a just epitaph.

They say: politicians are like monkeys; the higher they climb the pole of ambition, the more of their arses we can see!

Footnote by Evita Bezuidenhout

No, I'm sorry. Call me old-fashioned, but I just don't find politics funny. Looking at these drawings of P W and Pik and F W and the others whose names escape us all, I wonder: what was funny about what happened? I think too much is being made of this thing called satire. It's just not funny!

Although I was at first hurt, I'm now glad I have not been drawn in any of these cartoons. Ja – nee, I must have done something right!

iLegend

For Karina

10 March 1994

The prospect of democracy stirs Bophuthatswana*

*This and all other postscripts by Zapiro

17 March 1994   Eugene TerreBlanche describes the AWB's attempt to prop up Mangope as a 'brilliant victory'

23 March 1994

The tale of the Transitional Executive Council

NEGOTIATING IN LIQUID ASSETS

21 April 1994   As CODESA all-party talks continue, Buthelezi plays hard-to-get

9

26 April 1994

27 April 1994

Election Day

5 May 1994   A week till Inauguration Day, Judge Kriegler's Interim Electoral Commission is in the hot seat

12 May 1994

First day on the job

19 May 1994

New ministry, new Deputy Minister

LOOKING ACROSS THE BORDER

10 June 1994

8 June 1994   Minister of Justice Dullah Omar announces proposed commission

16

29 June 1994   Joe Slovo, Minister of Housing, inspects the Cape Flats

5 July 1994

6 July 1994   Minister of Finance Derek Keys resigns unexpectedly

7 July 1994

10 July 1994

21 July 1994 Minister Jay Naidoo runs the Reconstruction and Development Programme

25 July 1994   After a pre-Election bombing spree

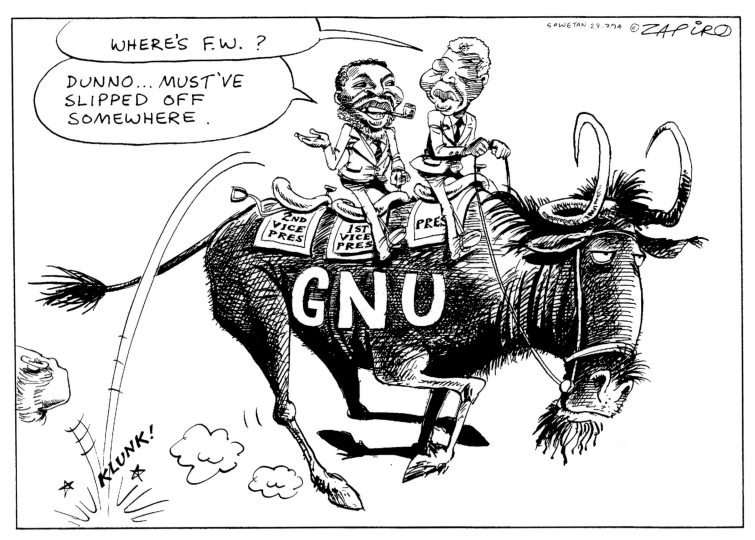

27 July 1994   He hasn't actually left the Government of National Unity. Yet.

28 July 1994

9 August 1994

11 August 1994   In Parliament Winnie Mandela makes a speech aiming to lay to rest the controversy surrounding the death of child-activist Stompie Sepei

18 August 1994

22 August 1994

29

15 September 1994   Debate on what to do with apartheid relics

IF YOUR POLITICAL CAREER IS ON THE SKIDS, AND YOU ARE IN DANGER OF BECOMING A LITTLE M...

MITTERRAND IN JULY

MUGABE IN AUGUST

MAJOR IN SEPTEMBER

....WHY NOT COME TO SUNNY SOUTH AFRICA, AND HAVE YOUR PHOTOGRAPH TAKEN WITH THE BIG M?

20 September 1994

21 September 1994   King Goodwill Zwelithini distances himself from Chief Mangosuthu Buthelezi, his uncle and long-time mentor

26 September 1994   Mangosutu and armed bodyguards storm into an SABC studio during an interview with Zwelithini's spokesperson. The ensuing scuffle is broadcast live on 'Agenda' …

29 September 1994

… following which, he is summoned to explain himself

34

6 October 1994

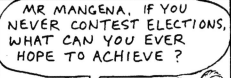

12 October 1994

"ANOTHER PAC FUNDRAISING DRIVE ?"

14 October 1994

13 October 1994

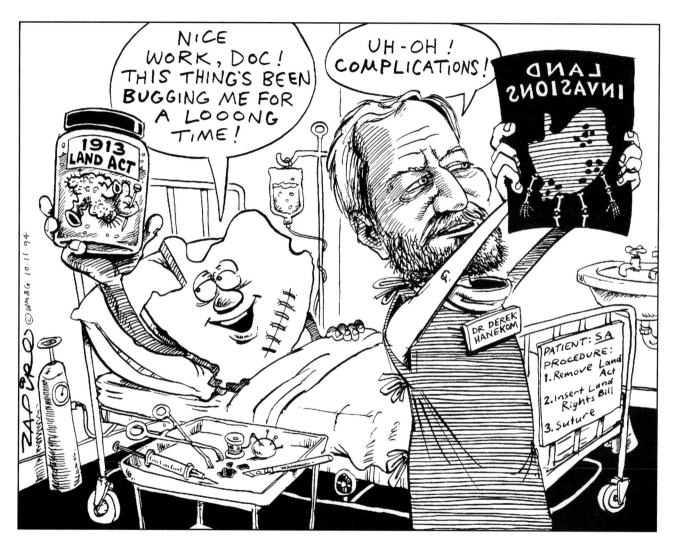

10 November 1994

6 December 1994

"...after climbing a great hill, one only finds that there are many more hills to climb."

—Nelson Mandela in "The Long Walk to Freedom".

15 December 1994   The President's long-awaited autobiography is published

20 December 1994   It's that time of year again …

18 January 1995   It turns out that, just before the '94 Election, Acting State President Pik Botha indemnified 3 000 former government functionaries, including big-guns Malan and Vlok

19 January 1995   The validity of the indemnity list (which also includes serving Police Commissioner Johan van der Merwe) is unclear

19 January 1995

... but it soon becomes clearer

30 January 1995

31 January 1995

Former security-policeman Craig Williamson starts talking

9 February 1995   Who, me? The Reverend Allan Boesak? Use funds for starving children for my own personal gain? The very thought!

8 February 1995

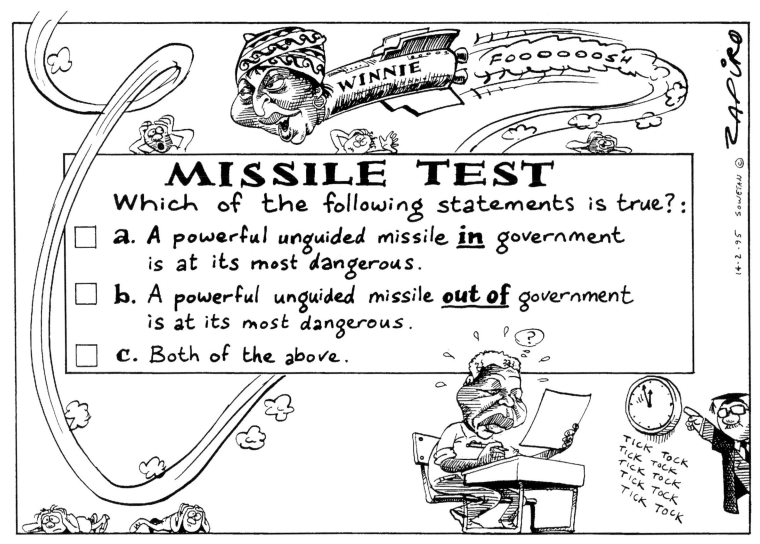

MISSILE TEST

Which of the following statements is true?:

☐ **a.** A powerful unguided missile **in** government is at its most dangerous.

☐ **b.** A powerful unguided missile **out of** government is at its most dangerous.

☐ **c.** Both of the above.

14 February 1995

50

THE RE-OPENING OF PARLIAMENT

17 February 1995

23 February 1995   Pushing for International Mediation in the Constitutional Negotiations, the IFP again uses its traditional weapon – the walkout

28 February 1995

23 March 1995

12 April 1995

What **else** does the Easter Bunny have to hide?

12 April 1995

30 March 1995

Winnie defies the President once too often

18 April 1995

19 April 1995

3 May 1995

I'm Deputy President Thabo Mbeki

60

12 May 1995

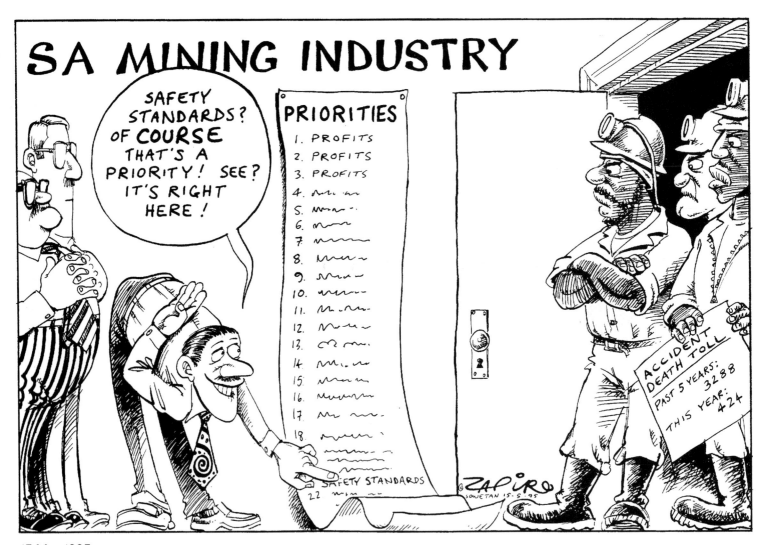

15 May 1995

17 May 1995

18 May 1995

1 June 1995   Constitutional Assembly Chairperson Cyril Ramaphosa consults the public

7 June 1995

12 June 1995

GREAT UNSOLVED MYSTERIES

The Curse of Tutankhamen

Bigfoot

The Bermuda Triangle

SA Foreign Policy

14 June 1995

After this cartoon, Alfred is burdened with many z's

THE JONAH LOMU QUIZ

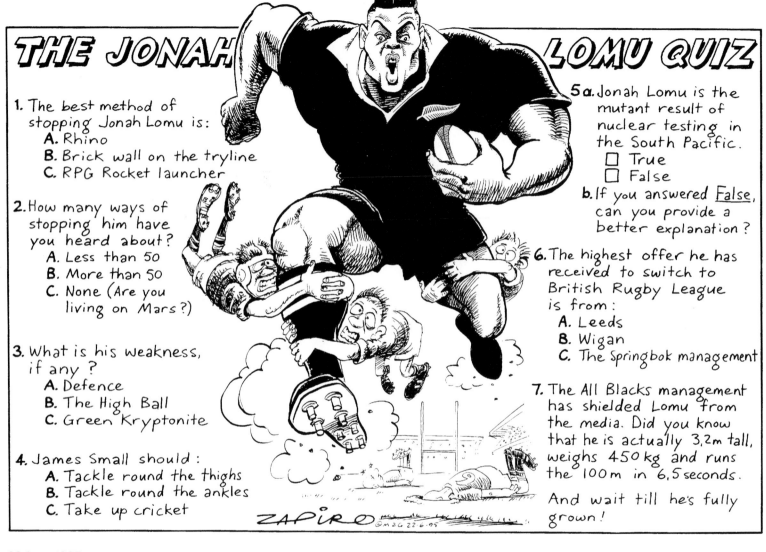

1. The best method of stopping Jonah Lomu is:
   A. Rhino
   B. Brick wall on the tryline
   C. RPG Rocket launcher

2. How many ways of stopping him have you heard about?
   A. Less than 50
   B. More than 50
   C. None (Are you living on Mars?)

3. What is his weakness, if any?
   A. Defence
   B. The High Ball
   C. Green Kryptonite

4. James Small should:
   A. Tackle round the thighs
   B. Tackle round the ankles
   C. Take up cricket

5a. Jonah Lomu is the mutant result of nuclear testing in the South Pacific.
   ☐ True
   ☐ False

   b. If you answered _False_, can you provide a better explanation?

6. The highest offer he has received to switch to British Rugby League is from:
   A. Leeds
   B. Wigan
   C. The Springbok management

7. The All Blacks management has shielded Lomu from the media. Did you know that he is actually 3.2m tall, weighs 450kg and runs the 100m in 6.5 seconds.

And wait till he's fully grown!

ZAPIRO ©M&G 22·6·95

22 June 1995

70

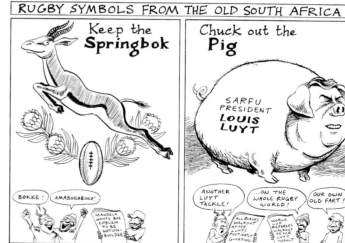

29 June 1995

10 July 1995

11 July 1995

2 August 1995

10 August 1995

17 August 1995

Seeking reconciliation

16 August 1995

22 August 1995

24 August 1995

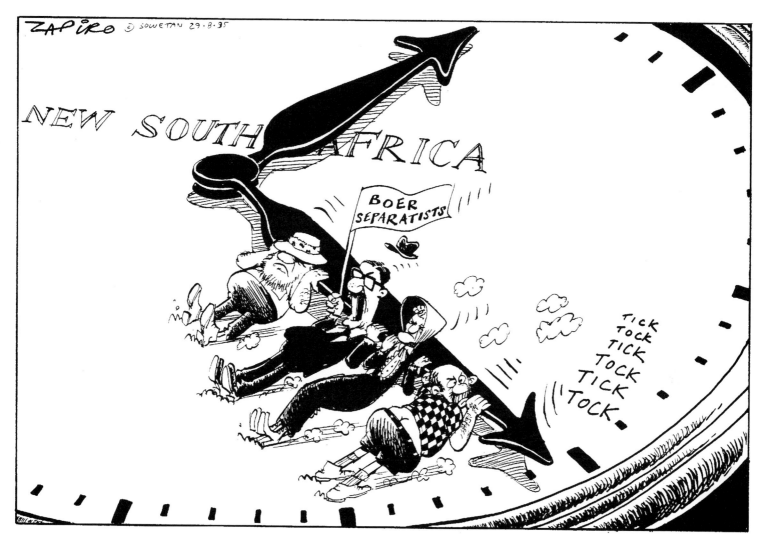

29 August 1995

4 September 1995

14 September 1995

Everybody's coming to South Africa, now that it's politically kosher

18 September 1995

31 October 1995   Magnus Malan and other generals are to stand trial for complicity in the KwaMakhutha Massacre committed by SADF-trained IFP militia

2 November 1995

Possible scenario

SOWETAN 6-11-95 ZAPIRO

6 November 1995

10 November 1995

22 November 1995

P W Botha: "Don't unleash the tiger in the Afrikaner"

28 November 1995   Winnie's umpteenth crisis, this time over kickbacks in her anti-poverty programme

8 December 1995

22 December 1995

19 January 1996

22 January 1996

...and they couldn't put Humpty together again.

18 January 1996

NATION-BUILDING IS A WHOLE NEW BALL GAME

SOWETAN 23-1-96© ZAPIRO

23 January 1996

25 January 1996

1 February 1996   Removal of apartheid relics from Parliament re-opens the debate about what to do with them

101

8 February 1996

19 February 1996

20 February 1996

GLIMMER OF HOPE

8 March 1996

The Malan trial begins. The De Kock trial has been going for some time.

107

5 March 1996

SARAFINA 2 QUIZ

©ZAPIRO
M&G 14·3·96

1. Which is more expensive?
   A. Bringing Broadway to Soweto.
   B. Taking Soweto to Broadway.

2. Which is bigger?
   A. The R14,2 million budget
   B. Mbongeni Ngema's ego

3. The Health Department's AIDS-education policy is:
   A. Throw money at the problem.
   B. Throw money at Mbongeni Ngema.

4. How has Dr Zuma responded to critics?
   A. Arrogance
   B. Indifference
   C. Racial red herrings
   D. All of the above

5. TENDERING PROCEDURE
   <u>What</u> tendering procedure?

6. TRANSPARENCY
   <u>What</u> transparency?

7. Which is hardest to find?
   A. The missing R1,1 million
   B. A humble word from Ngema
   C. An NGO consulted about the project

8. Which description of Sarafina 2 is most often used by AIDS experts?
   A. "hopelessly confused"
   B. "completely ineffective"
   C. "appalling"

14 March 1996

1962-1990

1990-1996

21 March 1996

2 April 1996

URBAN HANDSCAPE

3 April 1996   Private funders propose this R50-million, 23-metre high Mandela Monument. Seriously.

9 April 1996   Trevor Manuel is the first Minister of Finance to hail from the Liberation Movement

11 April 1996

18 April 1996

19 April 1996

25 April 1996

9 May 1996

Cyril presents the new constitution

119

This time it's for real

13 May 1996

Believe it or not....

16 May 1996

24 May 1996

WHICH HAS THE SHORTEST MEMORY SPAN?

A. mouse   **B.** flea

C. Western Cape voter who was oppressed by the Nats for 40 years, and happily votes Nat today.

29 May 1996   Cape Local Government Election

6 June 1996

11 June 1996   Stella Sicgau doesn't deny receiving the money when she was 'Prime Minister' of Transkei. "It was for my child's school fees" …

14 June 1996

4 July 1996

8 July 1996

130

11 July 1996

12 July 1996

15 July 1996

18 July 1996

16 July 1996

25 July 1996

30 July 1996

1 August 1996

5 August 1996   Bantu Holomisa alleges that his party, the ANC, accepted favours from Sol Kerzner in return for dropping bribery charges against Kerzner

140

7 August 1996

Trying to land the Big One

29 August 1996

142

8 September 1994

25 October 1994

17 November 1994

20 July 1995

French government anounces test plans

21 July 1995

8 May 1995

3 August 1995

Mugabe says homosexuals are 'worse than pigs and dogs'

7 August 1995

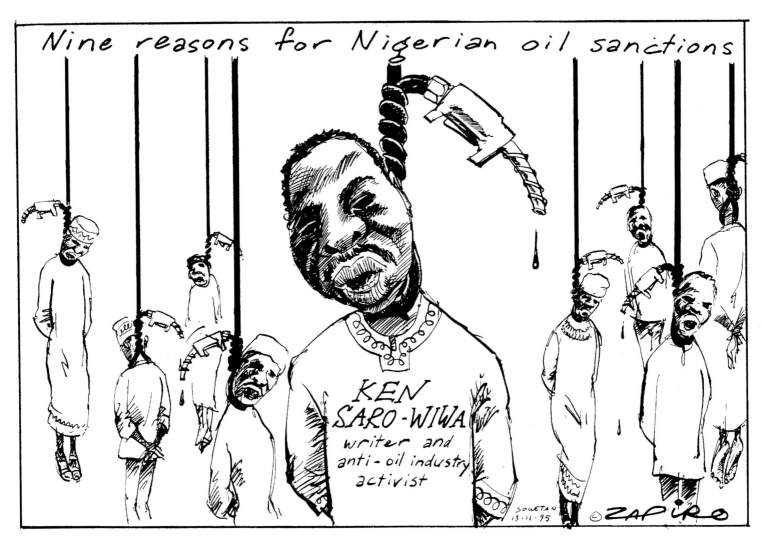

13 November 1995

30 November 1995

4 January 1996

26 March 1996

13 July 1994   Astronomers say Jupiter will be hit by devastating comets this week

18 July 1994

Italian disaster in the World Cup Final

"MR CARL GILES? YES, WE'RE EXPECTING YOU.... BUT WHO'S **THAT** CROWD?"

31 August 1995